WILLIAM WESTWOOD

Copyright © 2022 by Aidan Phelan

All rights reserved. No part of this book may be reproduced in any manner whatsoever without written permission except in the case of brief quotations embodied in critical articles and reviews.

The bulk of this book is taken from public domain material but has been curated and edited. Previous publications also exist containing portions of what is reproduced herein, but not in the form presented in this edition.

Selected sources: *Australasian (Melbourne)*, Saturday 1 February 1879, page 8; *Australasian (Melbourne)*, Saturday 8 February 1879, page 6; *Australasian (Melbourne)*, Saturday 15 February 1879, page 7; *Australasian (Melbourne)*, Saturday 22 February 1879, page 7; *Britannia and Trades' Advocate (Hobart Town, Tas. : 1846 – 1851)*, Thursday 29 April 1847, page 4; *Britannia and Trades' Advocate (Hobart Town, Tas. : 1846 – 1851)*, Thursday 5 November 1846, page 2; *Bell's Life in Sydney and Sporting Reviewer (NSW : 1845 – 1860)*, Saturday 28 November 1846, page 1; *Sentinel (Sydney, NSW : 1845 – 1848)*, Thursday 29 October 1846, page 2

Published by Australian Bushranging (Aidan Phelan)
Printed by IngramSpark

An entry for this text is available in the National Library of Australia database.

First Printing, 2022

ISBN (Print): 978-0-6489572-7-0
ISBN (eBook): 978-0-6489572-8-7

William Westwood

IN HIS OWN WORDS

William Westwood

Edited by Aidan Phelan

Australian Bushranging

Dedicated to the memory of William Westwood, whose powerful words encapsulated the tragedy of the convict era and warned us of the dangers of dehumanisation.

Contents

Preface	**1**
A Prelude by "Peutetre"	**13**
1 The Early Days	22
2 More Bushranging	33
3 Downfall	41
A Postscript by "Peutetre"	**51**
The Cooking Pot Riot	**55**
4 A Farewell to Family	67
5 The Last Letter	70
6 The Dying Declaration of William Westwood, alias "Jackey Jackey."	74
The Fate of William Westwood (as reported)	**75**

Preface

William Westwood, *alias* Jackey Jackey, is a bushranger that often gets overlooked in favour of his contemporary Martin Cash, or those who came after him such as Ben Hall and Ned Kelly, yet his is a fascinating story of adventure and tragedy worthy of recognition.

Westwood was born on 7 August 1820 and was raised in Manuden, Essex. He was the eldest of five siblings. At fourteen he had his first conviction: twelve months hard labour for bailing up a woman on the road and stealing clothes from her. Westwood's accomplice Ben Jackson got off comparatively lightly with a flogging.

After his release, Westwood was convicted again, this time for stealing a coat and pawning it. As this was his second offence, he was sentenced to be transported to Australia for fourteen years. Himself only sixteen, on 18 March 1837 Westwood departed England on Mangles to spend what would turn out to be the rest of his life on foreign soil.

He was a surprisingly bright and refined young man, with a reasonable education for the time and a strong grasp of language and eagerness to converse. He was described as standing at 5'5", with ruddy complexion, brown hair and grey eyes; a scar on the right side of his upper lip, another on the back of his right hand, a blister mark between the breasts and several tattoos — left arm: illegible blue mark, "7 Aug 1820" (his birthday), "3 Jan 1837" (the date his sentence was due to end); and a figure of the sun on the back of his left hand. The tattoos were likely either made while serving time in gaol or while waiting to be transported.

As will become evident in the following text, Westwood was surprisingly eloquent despite his lack of education. He could articulate his thoughts and feelings well, and this enabled him to record his memoirs. Unlike so many other bushrangers, Westwood's personal perspective on the life of a bush brigand has been preserved and provides an invaluable resource with which to learn.

When he arrived in New South Wales he was sent to Hyde Park Barracks and kept there until given his assignment. He was eventually assigned as a servant to Phillip King at Gidleigh Station, Bungendore. He would spend the next three years at Gidleigh under overbearing and tyrannical masters. He was always testing the boundaries, and after being spotted in town one night, having sneaked out of his quarters, was dragged back to Gidleigh and given fifty lashes. This only strengthened his resolve to rebel.

After suffering greatly at the hands of his master, who saw fit to have him beaten and whipped at even the slightest offence, as well as being short changed on his already inadequate supplies and rations by the overseer, in 1840 Westwood absconded again. When he was inevitably caught, he was given another fifty lashes and sent to work in an iron gang near Goulburn. Conditions here were even worse than at his first assignment, but he knew it would be fleeting and expected to be sent to a new assignment when he was done.

After his stint in the iron gang, he was sent back to Gidleigh, much to his dismay. The routine played out again: Westwood absconded, was caught and given fifty lashes. The next time, Westwood wanted to make sure he stayed at large. He and two other convicts gathered enough supplies to last them until they got clear away, then, on 14 December 1840, they bolted.

It wasn't long before Westwood fell in with the notorious bushranger Paddy Curran. The pair were associated from their time as convicts, and Westwood was eager to have a crack at bushranging. Curran was an extremely violent man compared to Westwood, and their morals were diametrically opposed in just about every way, but none so stark as their attitudes towards women. As the story goes, during a house raid, Westwood walked in on Curran in the process of raping the lady of the house. Westwood struck Curran and threatened to shoot him. Westwood decided he would rather work alone than associate with such a despicable person and they parted ways. Curran was hanged at Berrima Gaol on 21 October 1841 for the attempted murder of constable Patrick McGuire at the Black Range, Molonglo, and the rape of Mary Wilsmore at Bungendore.

As Westwood got the hang of highway robbery, news of his daring began to spread, though much of it was fiction. On one occasion it was said that he bailed up a commissary and upon discovering the commissary's wife was in the coach, opened the door, swept the ground with his cabbage tree hat in a gentlemanly manner and invited her to dance with him – a request that she obliged. This and many other anecdotes have no tangible evidence to back them up, however. Among his crimes, he robbed the Queanbeayan mail, and robbed Mr. Edinburgh among several others on the Sydney Road. In fact, he took a particular liking to robbing mailmen as the takings were often rather good.

Some accounts attested to his masterful horsemanship, likely honed while he worked as a groom at Gidleigh as part of his assignment. In one instance he reputedly bailed up a man in Goulburn and implored him to note the time, then a few hours later he bailed up another gentleman near Braidwood, almost 100 kilometers away, and implored him to do the same in order to set a personal record. His taste for racehorses was nigh on insatiable, with him stealing such creatures from Terrence Murray and several others in the region, either on the roads or from farms. He attributed his success in evading capture to his choice of fine horse flesh over the run-down nags the police rode.

On the afternoon of Monday 11 January 1841, Jacky Jacky stole a black mare from Mr. McArthur before attempting to rob a mailman that night at Bungonie, whereupon shots were fired. The next day he raided a store at Boro Creek where he procured fine garments and dressed himself in *haute couture* so that he may cut a fine figure while about his nefarious deeds, including a rather fetching top hat. Such was the extent of his outrages that the entirety of the mounted police in the region, trackers included, were led by Lieutenant Christie and a Mr. Stewart in hot pursuit.

On 13 January 1841, things came to a head when a man arrived in Bungendore, shouting that he was being chased by a bushranger who meant to shoot him. Sure enough, Jacky Jacky soon arrived on a stolen horse, riding through Bungendore for fully an hour and a half, stopping only to have a chat with a man named Eccleston. Soon word reached the local magistrate, Powell, who went with his brother Frank and a local man named Richard Rutledge to capture the infamous bushranger, despite a distinct lack of weapons with which to defend themselves against the armed bandit. Alas after the posse hesitated in approaching the rogue, he caught wind of them and mounted his steed, riding off at full gallop. The men gave chase. A man named William Balcombe was riding ahead with

Revered McGrath in a gig. Stopping the gig in the road, McGrath and Balcombe got out and Balcombe confronted the bushranger, McGrath also pulling a revolver on him. Westwood surrendered, complaining that he could have gotten away if his musket were not in such poor shape.

The desperado was escorted back to the local inn where he was detained. However, he was not ready to go down without a fight and during the night he overpowered one of his guards and stole his weapons. He bolted out of the inn and across the plains. This did not go un-noticed, and Frank Powell saw the fugitive legging it through the open space. Powell fired a pistol at Westwood without effect and gathered more firearms from inside before heading off in pursuit with a postman who had become embroiled in the affair by accident. Soon the notorious Jacky Jacky was once more apprehended, but the next day while being escorted to Bargo Brush, Westwood escaped custody on foot. He made it a mile away before being recaptured. Not in the mood for any nonsense, the police tied Westwood to his horse for the remainder of the trip. That night, Westwood broke out of the lock up and stole the guard's weapon and ammunition before taking a horse and riding to freedom.

The beginning of the end came when he called into the Black Horse Inn on the Berrima Road. Westwood casually walked in and ordered refreshments. He then proceeded to bail the place up. Folklore tells that he was served by Miss Gray, the publican's daughter, who recognised him from his pistol braces and fine clothes. She screamed and pounced on the bushranger, who fought to throw the girl off as she called for her mother and father. All three tried to restrain Westwood who shook them off time and again until a man named Waters, a carpenter that had been repairing shingles on the inn's roof, entered and knocked Westwood out cold by striking him on the head with a shingling hammer. In truth it was Grey, the publican, and two assigned servants, Waters and McCrohan, who subdued the bushranger, who took two fierce blows to the head with the shingling hammer to go down, which miraculously didn't kill him. With Westwood captured, the Grays earned themselves a cool £30 reward and Westwood was quickly locked up in Wooloomooloo Gaol.

He was put on trial for robbing the store at Boro and was sentenced to penal servitude for life and sent to Darlinghurst Gaol but was shortly caught trying to escape. He was then imprisoned on Cockatoo Island where he organised a party of twenty-five other convicts to join him in an escape attempt. The gang subdued a guard and tied him up. Breaching the boundaries, they made it to the water and were about to risk sharks and drowning to swim to Balmain but were captured by the water police. Westwood was then sent to fulfill his sentence at Port Arthur in Van Diemen's Land with his co-conspirators.

By some accounts, while being sent to Tasmania, the convict men were put in the brig of the prison ship, naked and shackled to prevent any attempts to escape. This failed and the men broke free from their cages and tried to reach the deck. Soldiers battened down the hatches and kept the men trapped until arrival at Port Arthur. When the hatches were opened the prisoners were unconscious in the brig, having been denied food and adequate oxygen due to the captain's decision not to risk opening the hatches to take food to the men during the several days trip.

Despite Port Arthur's reputation at the time as an inescapable prison, William Westwood managed to escape from Port Arthur multiple times. Most occasions resulted in a few days of "freedom" at most stumbling through the bush. In one attempt at freedom with two other convicts, the trio waded naked into the waters at Eaglehawk Neck. Westwood's companions were taken by sharks and he was found days later wandering lost, naked and starving.

Such repeated misbehaving saw him put in solitary confinement for almost three months. When he emerged he was assigned to the commissariat. At this time, he helped rescue a boatload of soldiers after their vessel had capsized. His reward was to be sent to Glenorchy Probation Station. Here, as could be anticipated, he once more escaped on 31 July 1845. This time he successfully took to bushranging with two others. They travelled up through the Tasmanian Midlands, attempting to reach Launceston where they planned to steal a boat and sail to Sydney. They became hopelessly lost and were unable to find a boat, resulting in one of the men leaving their company after getting lost, while the other remained until they reached Green Ponds, whereupon he left for fear that Westwood would shoot him as he was the designated guide through the bush and had only succeeded in getting them stranded in unfamiliar territory. When Westwood found himself alone again, he continued, on foot, towards Launceston, hoping to find a way off the island, but was recaptured before reaching his destination. By this time, he was suffering a bout of deep depression and posed no resistance.

Now having exasperated the Van Diemen's Land government too, he was sentenced to death. The penalty was altered to penal servitude for life on Norfolk Island and Westwood found himself once more sailing to exile, this time headed to what was referred to as the Isle of Despair.

In February of 1844, there was a change of administration at Norfolk Island. Alexander Maconochie, the previous man in charge, had firmly believed in the benefits of rehabilitating offenders rather than simply punishing them, and to this end he reduced work hours, including a work-free Sunday, and created a "marks" system that meant that good behaviour would be rewarded. Flogging incidents were decreased but still strictly enforced in cases of sodomy, which were rampant throughout the prison. Perhaps the most significant measure Maconochie had brought in was vegetable patches. Inmates were given small gardens within which they could grow their own sweet potatoes and other vegetables and were also given cooking pots and utensils so that they could cook their own meals, allowing them to eat in their cells in privacy. Only able to enact these reforms with the 600 newest inmates, the reforms were still considerably effective, with morale high and major incidents in the prison reduced. Despite Governor Gipps' recommendations to the government to continue Maconochie's residency at Norfolk Island, the decision had already been made and Major Joseph Childs became the new Commandant.

As a military man with wide campaign experience, and a strict disciplinarian, Childs decided to institute a few changes to bring the convicts under his thumb. To this end incidents of flogging were increased, hours of labour were also increased, rations were reduced and the small gardens the prisoners were allowed, and the produce they had been growing therein, were banned. In a half-hearted attempt to respond to complaints the administration allowed convicts a cup of peas and a cup of flour every day. Unsurprisingly this was not met with the gratitude that was expected by the administration and Childs set in place a proclamation whereby food was to be served in bulk and individual cooking was prohibited. When the inmates were away from their cells, on 1 July 1846, their utensils were confiscated.

This was the final straw and Westwood incited a work party to take up arms against the guards and administration of the island. Approximately 1,600 inmates joined in. Armed with an axe, Westwood claimed four lives in the mayhem – an overseer and three constables. After managing to escape, the commandant roused a force of troops that descended upon the marauders and subdued them.

Westwood and thirteen other key figures in the riot, including bushranger Lawrence Kavanagh, formerly of Cash and company, were tried in September and charged with the murder of John Morris, formerly a gatekeeper at Port Arthur. The evidence was irresistible and twelve of the men were sentenced to execution by hanging. No convictions were made in respect of the other murders as the result of the Morris case was deemed sufficient. On 13 October 1846, William Westwood was hanged for his crimes. He was twenty-six years old.

***

The inclusion of the introduction and afterword by "Peutetre" - the *nom de plume* of Thomas George Rogers - is to contextualise the autobiography, its author and how it came to be. Rogers was an Irishman who was appointed to the position of religious instructor to the convicts at Norfolk Island in 1844, in which capacity he encountered Westwood. Over the time he spent on the island, Rogers complained about the inhumane treatment of the convicts under the administration of Joseph Childs. Rogers even went so far as to report Childs to the Colonial Office and it is hardly a surprise that he felt it was appropriate to have Westwood's autobiography published to showcase the torment convicts were put through on account of the overbearing and cruel officials put in charge of the penal settlements. He continued to be a champion for the convicts, playing an instrumental part in the creation of the Anti-Transportation League.

It is not indicated by his words, nor indeed from the contemporary records of his actions as a bushranger in the years prior, that Westwood was capable of the callousness and violence that led him to the gallows. He was noted for the way he avoided violence, but the severity of conditions on Norfolk Island had clearly worn him down to his last nerve and in the end he claimed four lives as compensation for his torment.

Westwood addressed his final letter, written just moments before being led to the gallows, to the Reverend Edward Durham who had evidently shown considerable humanity to Westwood and some of the other men that were set to hang that had been inmates at Port Arthur. Durham was the first occupant of the parsonage at Port Arthur, where he lived and worked for many years. He frequently clashed with the site's commandant Charles O'Hara Booth, particularly over the treatment of the convicts. Booth seemed to consider Durham to be nothing but a madman.

It is unsurprising that with the religious leaders in these penal settlements being the only men standing up for the treatment of convicts as human beings that they would be viewed as meddlesome by the authorities and held in high regard by convicts. Certainly, Westwood seems to have embraced his faith in prison likely as a result of the benevolence offered to him by the likes of Durham and Rogers. His religiousness is on full display in his final letters, perhaps in an effort to put his parents' mind to rest about the state of his soul in the hereafter. There is little reason to doubt that he was earnest in his faith.

That Westwood not only decided to expend his last moments writing to Durham, but to speak on behalf of the other men who may have wished to convey their sentiments to the reverend but lacked the capacity, is indicative of the powerful effect even the slightest humanity had on the convicts who had endured the great evils of the penal system.

Ultimately, Westwood's life stands as a testament to the effects of systemic cruelty on the mind and body, and the hideous barbarity of a system that maims and tortures men to break their spirit rather than reform them. When Westwood became a convict, he was a child and in his few, fleeting adult years he never knew a life where he wasn't either incarcerated or trying to avoid capture, and, in the end, he craved the sweet release of death. He had been reduced to little more than a wild animal; hunted and harassed then caged and exterminated. But with his own words he can tell his story in a way that allows him to reclaim his humanity and campaign for a world where a small transgression need not be a life sentence, and a young man ambling down the wrong path in life can be steered onto the right path through compassion and benevolence instead of brute force.

Aidan Phelan

A Prelude by "Peutetre"

The narrative, to which these remarks are introductory, which has been handed to us by a contributor, is of interest as presenting the incidents and motives of a bushranger's life from a point of view from which it is seldom seen. It is unnecessary to point out the "personal equation" which has to be allowed for in the writer's statement of his actions, resulting partly from that desire to put forward a justification of some sort or other which is shown by the greatest criminals, and partly from the vanity and mock-heroism which seem usually to be conspicuous elements in the characters of highwaymen of all times. These allowances we may safely leave to the reader. We wish here merely to mention that we have satisfied ourselves of the perfect authenticity of the narrative, and now leave our contributor to explain how the document came into his hands. He gives the following account "How I Came By It":—

I do not believe there is a word of fiction in the following narrative. It is no made-up story, fancifully exaggerated, but a very unadorned, and straightforward tale of audacious bushranger adventure and privation, in which a young outlaw relates in his own way the incidents of his brigand career in two colonies. These incidents he describes without bravado or self-glorification, and with slight excuses for his lawless exploits. His rustic habits and limited education did not qualify him to write with any view to stage effect; yet the scenes he delineates, and in which he was a chief actor, are full of wild robber – daring and dramatic *pose*, and have all the interest that attaches to bold and reckless deeds of actual occurrence.

The recent tragic events near Mansfield will serve to show with what fatal facility such deeds may be done in half-reclaimed woodland regions, and how a few desperadoes like the Kellys can terrify a whole district for many months together, and plunder or destroy life with impunity, even in times when mounted police and well-made roads are by no means so few and far between as in the dark ages of Australia five and thirty years ago, and before Victoria was born. In those dark and less settled times, the "Bolters" were a very dangerous substitute in the bush for royal Bengal tigers, though the thirst of blood in these human beasts of prey does not seem to have much abated since the convict era; for what Siberian wolf could ravin for and lap up gore with keener appetite than Morgan, or what old Sydney "cockatoo" or Port Arthur "canary" could more treacherously assassinate than the gang which has now so long baffled the whole gendarmerie of this country? Unlike so many of the class, the hero of this present bush romance had few of the exterior marks and tokens about him of the brutal and ferocious marauder. He was a young man of six and twenty, of good stature, broad-chested, and muscular in limb, though not of brawny build, but lithe and agile as a leopard. He was of a fair complexion, regular features, and a good humoured expression of countenance, to which a broad forehead gave an air of intelligence. This broad forehead was overhung with a profusion of straw-coloured hair of a dark shade. He had a pleasant smile, which disclosed two rows of small white teeth, so small and so white as to give him a somewhat feminine appearance, which was made more feminine by thin red lips, small mouth, and well-shaped chin. But the most noticeable of all his features were his eyes, which were deep set and of a rich violet blue. I never saw eyes more "deeply, darkly, beautifully blue," that is, in his ordinary and placid mood; but when roused to anger their mild soft violet hue wholly vanished, and in its place came something that flushed and glowed like two red coals. I first discovered this ocular transformation by coming one day unexpectedly to his cell in the new gaol at Norfolk Island when he was having a verbal altercation with the turnkeys who had annoyed him. I scarcely recognised him. The usual smile had given way to a frightful scowling frown, and his eyes seemed literally turned into two balls of fire, reminding me of Sir Walter Scott's description in Ivanhoe of Richard Coeur-de-lion's eyes when that warrior king was pleased to lash himself up to a frenzy of rage.

Our outlaw, however, was not of a peevish or quarrelsome temper, and took no delight in giving his officers trouble, as others often did, in neglecting his work, nor did he mix himself up with the common squabbles of the Lumber-yard. His demeanour at Norfolk Island was inoffensive until the unlucky morning of the July riot, in which several of the civil officers were injured and four constables killed — three of them by the hand of our outlaw, Westwood. A long series of disciplinary severities, and some vexatious alterations and reductions in the legal allowance of food, had produced extreme discontent amongst the prisoners, especially on the Settlement Station, where they numbered about 800. The Government store was sometimes nearly bankrupt in flour, meal, beef, sugar, and potatoes; and the dietary of "the men" was regulated according to the state of the store. Sundry refusals of the gangs to go to work half-fed were only succeeded by more stringent measures of coercion, until the prisoners were galled and exasperated beyond their bearing. The last ounce of sand that broke the camel's back was laid on by an order to take away from the mess-sheds some 40 or 50 old kettles in which "the men" had for several years been permitted to boil water, and make maize corn coffee after coming in from the fields and quarries, A mutiny and a murderous attack on the constables resulted, in which our outlaw took the lead, and for this he was tried and sentenced to death at a special Norfolk Island assizes, held by a judge sent down from Hobart Town, assisted by five military officers of the garrison, who sat with the judge as assessors.

This autobiography was chiefly written by our outlaw while awaiting trial; a page or two were added after his condemnation, and all of it, except in the spelling, remains as he penned it. I passed the last night of his mortal life with him in his cell, in which two other men, also under sentence, were present. It was a night to be remembered. Sleep came not to the eyelids which were so soon to close for ever; nor drowsiness to men whose wakeful hearts were pondering on the dread mysterious secrete which the grave would unfold to them upon the morrow. Yet, although subdued, they were not dejected. They were even cheerful, and disposed for conversation, and I think if any one had been with them who would have spoken to them of a plan for getting off the island they would have eagerly discussed it for half the night; for the first and last thought of a prison is liberty — escape.

When the cell door was bolted on us, and the gaol-yard locked for the night, a painful stillness seemed to come down and gather round us with a stifling oppressiveness, and for a few minutes we all sat silent, as if listening for some sound or voice that might assure us of our proximity to living beings. We seemed as though entombed in a charnel-house. But the only sound that came was the booming roar of the South Pacific Ocean hurling its massy waves upon the coral reefs, over which they tumbled and fell with a foaming crash along the narrow beach close by the prison walls, which vibrated with the concussion. From this short stupor the chaplain gently recalled the men, inviting them to religious discourse and to acts of devotion until midnight. Free and friendly converse then ensued for a while, and the three doomed ones spoke of various passages in their penal life, mingling frequent, though not boisterous, laughter with many quaint and witty comments on their own and others' doings or misdoings.

About an hour after midnight our candles had burned low, and the task of lighting fresh ones was undertaken by Truelock, the oldest of the three men. In performing this task some burning wick fell on the back of his hand, and the grimaces he made in his hurried efforts to dislodge it were so comical his companions laughed merrily at them, and their laughter was increased by the grave tone and solemn shake of his head with which he reproved their mirth. "Men," he said," you should remember this is no time for grinning, at a fellow-creature's sufferings, when you are to be hanged at 8 o'clock this very morning." After this the chaplain, who was one of the highest of high church-men, addressed some words of exhortation to his small flock assembled in that cell on the duty of confessing their sins. Westwood, he found, was of the Church of England; another was a Wesleyan; and the third a Baptist; after half-an-hour's explanation, the chaplain entreated of them to review their lives and confess all their sins penitently to God, and then he would "give them absolution." The men then bowed their heads upon their knees as they sat in heavy chains, and in perfect silence so continued for a quarter of an hour. Then the chaplain rose up, and laying his hands on the head of the Baptist youth, Henry Whiting, he pronounced the absolution formula as given in the Anglican Prayer Book for the sick or dying; next he bestowed the same benefit on the Wesleyan, and, lastly, on Westwood, who seemed very devout.

Another hour was then employed in prayers, and as these were ended Whiting, who was only 22 years of age, looked sharply up to the little grating over the cell door. We all turned our eyes in the same direction, and lo, the dull grey glimmer of the wintry dawn was faintly visible. It seemed to me as the eye of the angel of death grimly looking in upon his victims. They gazed upon it long and silently, and at last he whose quick eye first detected it turned to me, and with a smile so sad, so wistful, and so pensive that it has never left my mind, he said, "Mr. Peutetre, it is the last!"

Our outlaw continued to watch the slowly growing light, as if his thoughts were faraway in his native home, among his kindred, beneath his father's roof, with sisters and brothers who knew not that he was going forth that selfsame day to a death of infamy. While Westwood was still gazing upwards at the light, the garrison bugles sounded the reveille, which led the chaplain to speak of the judgment trumpet, and then engaged once more in prayer. As this prayer ended the bell of the prisoners' barracks hard by began to ring. They all adverted to the well-known summons which had so often called them forth to their daily toil.

"It is tolling for our funeral," said Truelock. "Aye," responded Whiting; "it's our death knell!"

Shortly after the barrack bell had ceased its harsh jangle the footsteps of the turnkey were heard approaching. The bolt of our cell door was withdrawn, and a welcome sea breeze came whirling in upon us with its saline odours and refreshing dullness. But something still more welcome soon entered. The chaplain's wife and other ladies had sent down a basket well filled with cold fowl and ham and eggs, and well-buttered bread, and a can of coffee for the dying men's last breakfast. Plates and mugs were soon filled and handed round to those for whom they were provided. Did not the thought of the ropes dangling from the gallows erected within 20 yards of them spoil their appetite? Apparently it did not. In spite of rope, and heavy chains, and coarse white cap, they ate with seeming relish, and even with jocularity. While I was handing an additional slice of ham to Whiting, whose pathetic exclamation, "it is the last," had so touched me, he said, What a pity it is, men, that we aren't to be hanged every morning, if the ladies would only send us such jolly fine breakfasts," at which the "men" laughed heartily, as they did at one or two other ludicrous trifles that occurred while eating their last meal on earth.

Shortly after the repast was finished the sheriff came and ordered their chains to the struck off, so that they might ascend the ladder to the platform. Whiting and then Truelock had been led out for this purpose, and as I stood alone with Westwood in the cell, who was waiting for his turn, he drew a roll of paper from his breast, and said "Mr. Peutetre, I give you this — all I have to give. If ever you go back to old England, give the letters and the hair inside to my father and mother. God bless you and farewell." He was then called to have his chains struck off. This was how I came by his autobiography; and this is why I think it no fiction. Almost every statement made in it was proved on his trials; and many persons must still be living who will remember *Jacky Jacky*, which, perhaps, is a corruption of *Jika Jika*. I forgot to ask him how and why he got or took his bushranger title.

As an instance of the perils to which peaceful households were exposed, and also as a sample of the highly melodramatic situations to which the inburst of bushrangers sometimes gave rise, I would mention the following:— Jacky Jacky (Westwood) states that he and Gilling and Allom bailed up a station a few miles above New Norfolk, in Tasmania. After I left Norfolk Island I was on duty for some time at New Norfolk. One day riding with the police magistrate, we were invited to luncheon at Mr. H.'s, J.P., when his wife asked me about Jacky Jacky, saying she had once had the pleasure of being bailed up by him. It was in the Christmas holidays and her brother, Mr. Stanley J., of Hobart Town, and two other gentlemen, had come to stay a few days with her husband. On the first day of their visit, after dinner, some of the gentlemen went upstairs to have a nap until tea-time. She had retired to the drawingroom, and was employing herself at her workbox. By and bye her brother came into the room, and sat down in the rocking — "the chair you are now sitting in, Mr. Peutetre," said the lady. Leaning back in the chair, he said to her, "Well, I declare to you, Bessy, I never spent a happier day than this. I really never was so happy in all my life; nev—." Here he paused abruptly, and Mrs. H. turned her head to see what had cut his rocking and his enthusiastic speech so short, and found him staring in mute amazement towards the drawingroom door. Glancing in the same direction, to her astonishment and terror she beheld a tall young man, with sunburnt face, standing in the doorway with a double-barrelled gun in his hands, levelled point blank at the body of the happy brother, Mr. S. J., in the happiest moment of his whole life; the said tall sunburnt young man (Westwood) being prepared to fire on the happy gentleman, if he attempted to stand up. No sensational play could arrange a more theatrical scene than this startling impromptu reality in Mrs. H's drawingroom.

PEUTETRE.

1

The Early Days

I was bred and born in Manuden, in Essex. I was brought up by a kind father and mother. They tried to give me a good education, but I paid no attention to it. I entered upon evil courses when very young. At 16 years of age, I was taken up for highway robbery, and was committed to Chelmsford gaol in 1835. On the day of trial, through the intercession of my father, and on account of my youth, I got off with 12 months' imprisonment. When my time had expired, on the morning I was released from gaol, the first person I saw was my father waiting to accompany me home, where on arriving I was surrounded with kindness by my parents, and my father advised me never again to keep company with my old companions. I took his advice for some time, but not for long. I became acquainted with a young man, a greater vagabond than myself, who induced me to live like himself, by plunder both by day and by night. But this game did not last long. It brought me among my old companions and to Chelmsford gaol.

On January 3, 1837, I was tried for robbery, and, being an old offender, received 14 years' sentence of transportation, while my companion was discharged. While I remained in gaol, waiting to go down to Portsmouth, one day I shall never forget, my father and mother, and sisters and brothers, came to take their last farewell of me. The tears rolled down their cheeks for their undutiful son and bad brother. I took my leave of them at the time, thinking I never should see them anymore. Shortly afterwards I was removed down to Portsmouth, and had been there only a few days when an order came down from London for 300 prisoners to go on board the ship Mangles, and I was one among the number. We sailed from Portsmouth March 15, 1837, and had a pleasant voyage (to Sydney). Soon after landing I was assigned to a gentleman in the interior of the country, a very hard and severe man. He did not allow me a sufficiency of food, and only a scanty supply of clothing. I had not been with him long when I was prosecuted several times for little or nothing. I found it impossible to remain with him and I took the bush, thinking to make my situation in life better; I was well aware I could not make it any worse. Through my not knowing the bush I was soon taken by the mounted police and brought back to my master again, after I had been tied up and received 50 lashes. I now made up my mind never to remain with him. I took the bush again, but was soon captured and sent to court, and sentenced to six months in a chain gang. I now thought within myself that I was rid of my master, but to my great mistake, when my six months in the chain gang were done, I was sent back to him once more.

I was now put to a standstill. I did not see what to do. I did not fancy stopping with him to be starved to death in the land of plenty. One night me and two other men went out and committed a robbery with arms in order to supply our wants, and things went on in this way for some considerable time. I had enough of everything I wanted. My master looked jealous, but he did not know how it was done, as I worked for him in the day, but worked for myself in the night. But, at last, I was bowled out. One night, with my two companions, a robbery was committed, and the next day we were taken up on suspicion and brought before a magistrate. My two companions were committed for trial, and I was discharged and again sent back to my old; master. In the course of two or three days I was told that one of my mates had turned King's evidence, and I knew I might as well take the bush and have a run for it, as I was well aware I might expect to be transported, if not hanged. That night I bolted, with the intention of taking arms, and the first place I made for was one of my master's sheep stations, to see one of my old farm mates.

I had not been long there when I heard the noise of a horse's feet come galloping up to the hut. I ran to the door to see who it was, and who should it be but a man I knew very well, who had been in the bush about 18 months. He was a terror to the settlers in that part of the country, and was well mounted and armed. He dismounted and came into the hut. I liked his appearance very much. I got into a yarn with him and told him how I was situated, and that I liked his line of life, and would serve with him as his companion if he was willing. He looked at me, but gave me no answer. I then got up and went over to him and took his hand, and said, "Here is my band and my heart to go with you if you like." He hesitated a little, and then said I could come. So, we bid the hutkeeper good day, and off we went together through the bush until we came to a road. Here my companion dismounted and tied his horse to a tree, and then concealed myself alongside of I the road ready to receive the first traveller that came by.

We had not been there long when I saw a horseman come riding along. When he came close up me and my companion jumped out into the centre of the road, and my companion cried out, "Stand;

don't move hand or foot, or I'll blow your brains out. Get off that horse. Have you got any money?" The traveller got off, and I went up and searched him. I took £7 from his pockets and the watch off his neck. Then we led him and his horse a short way among the trees, where I ordered him to strip. He did not understand this, but I soon explained that I wanted his clothes, and in return I would give him mine. His were just my fit, and then I mounted his horse, which was a good one. We bid him good-day, and off we went full gallop. When night came on, we camped out, and the next morning we went to stick up a settler's place about a mile distant.

We rode up to the house, and stuck them nil up. After searching the men, we ordered the mistress of the housed to get us some refreshment, which she did. After a good snack, and drinking a couple of bottles of wine, I went outside to look at the horses. While outside I heard a scream, and ran inside, where I saw my companion attempting some liberties with the mistress of the House. I checked him at once; when he drew a pistol from his belt, and was levelling it at me when I rushed upon him and struck it out of his hand. This led to a row between us, and I resolved to part from such a hot-tempered companion, as two of the same sort were better asunder. I left him there, and mounting my horse I went off by myself.

I was now left alone to manage a trade I did not much understand, but my heart was good to learn. I now was my own master, and it was my wish to remain so. I came out on a road after a long ride, and determined to stick up the first passenger that came. I had not been there very long when I saw a man come riding along, When close up I jumped out into the middle of the road, and used the word of command as I heard it from my companion yesterday, "Stand; don't move hand or foot, or I'll blow your brains out. What have you got in them leather bags before you on your saddle?" "They are the mailbags, sir," he said; but there's nothing in them but letters." "How do you know what's in them; unbuckle them and throw them from your saddle. Quick! I'll soon see what's in them." On overhauling the bags I found, to my great satisfaction, they contained something else besides letters. I unsealed several and found they had money in them. I then mounted my horse, and set off about a mile with the bags, where I dismounted and searched the swag. It took me some time to open such a number of letters. The sum I found in them was £70, and cheques and orders £200. After this I was always very partial to mailmen.

At this time Christmas was close at hand, and I went to a friend of mine, as I took him to be. At his place I was made welcome, and he appeared happy to see me. Two days before Christmas Day I gave him some money to go to a store and buy some rum and other things to make merry Christmas with. In the afternoon, by chance, I took a walk to meet him on his return. At length I saw him coming, and five constables with him. I concealed myself in the trees and let them go on, laughing in my sleeve to think how nicely they were sharped. My horse was up at his place, but that made small odds, as I could soon get another. I made for the main road to get a nag, as I did not fancy walking. When I got to the road, I stationed myself to receive the first swell that came. After a while I saw two gentlemen come riding together, engaged in a deep yarn; when close I rushed out, shouting to them to stand or be shot. They seemed quite astonished at my sudden command; but I ordered them to dismount and tie their horses to a tree, and then demanded their money, and made them turn out their pockets. They turned out £19 between them. Picking up this I mounted one of their horses, bid them good day, and pushed off into the bush.

My next attempt was on a settler's house. I rode up to it, and bid the master of it good day. He made me no answer, and did not relish the looks of me, for he seemed frightened. There were four men on the farm besides himself. I bailed them all up, making one man tie the other. Next, I ordered the woman-servant to bind the master's hands behind his back. All were now secured but the females, and these I wanted to wait on me. I now overhauled the place, and the first thing I saw was a double-barrel piece and a brace of pistols, and grasped them eagerly. The next thing that drew my attention was one of the men singing out to me, "For God's sake, don't rob my master, for he is a good man," winking his eye at me the same time, as much as to say, he is a great vagabond. I next ordered the females to get me some refreshment as quick as possible, and after that I had a glass or two of wine. Then I untied the master's hands, and made him load one of his own horses with a sackful of everything I required. I then mounted my own horse, and led the pack-horse by my side. I made for the mountains to have a spell, as the police were now rather busy. The country for me. I remained in ambush as long as my store lasted.

When this was done, I thought it was time to have another parley with the mailmen. So, I mounted my horse, and made for the road between Goulburn and Yass. At 4 o'clock in the afternoon the mail made its appearance. I rode up full gallop in front of the driver, and cried out, "Pull up, or I'll blow your head off," keeping a strict eye on the passengers at the same time. "Come down one and all, and be quick. Now turn out your pockets," was the word; and then ordering them to stand back, and I put the contents of their pockets into my pocket. I next ordered them to stand back a distance of 100 yards, while I overhauled the mail. I dismounted and got up on the coach. I took the mail bags from the box, and likewise a carpetbag. I buckled them in the front of my saddle, mounted my horse, and bid them good day, and I turned mailman. After I had got about a mile in the bush, I rummaged the bags, and was employed for an hour in breaking letters open. The total sum of money the different letters contained amounted to £200. With this I thought I might as well take a trip down to Sydney. It was dangerous to remain in that part of the country, for the police were everywhere. The country was in a complete uproar after me.

I dung my horse, and took the coach down to Sydney. When I reached Sydney, I put up at a hotel in George street. I remained in Sydney about a month, regaling myself with every kind of sport. One night when I was at the play, I observed a man looking at me very hard as if he knew me. I recognised him to be a shipmate of mine, who came with me in the Mangles from England. I left the theatre and got out of Sydney as fast as I could. When I got up the country everything was very quiet. I thought it was time to give them another stir up, as they seemed so dull. I commenced again by sticking the first swell up who came the road. I had not been waiting long before Mr. P. M. arrived. I received him with open arms and the usual salute, "Stand; don't move hand or foot, or I'll blow your brains out." He looked like a stuck pig. And the next word was, "Come off that horse. Now, turn out your pockets." He turned out about £30; and then I cried, "Hand that watch this way." He had a splendid suit of clothes on, which were about my fit. I took him into the bush a short distance, and made him strip. I took his clothes and gave him mine. After he had dressed himself, I struck a light and lit my pipe, and got into a great yarn with him about the affairs of the country. I handed him a cigar, and he had a smoke. After we had done smoking, I tied his horse to a tree, and took him with me to the side of the road, waiting to receive the next visitor that came that way. By and bye I saw two gentlemen coming on horseback. When they came up to where I was concealed, I sprang out, crying, "Stand, or I'll blow your heads off." "Pray, don't hurt us, sir," said the gentlemen. I made them dismount and turn out their pockets, and I got £11 between them. I now picked the best horse out, and mounted him. He was as lively as a bag of fleas. Then I bid them good-bye, and off I went. As I was riding through the bush,

I saw three mounted policemen, well-armed. When they saw me they put spurs to their horses, and made towards me full gallop. I put spurs to my horse, and off he went like the wind. The further they came after me the further they got behind; and I soon gave them the go-by.

The next place I made for was Mr. Cardoe's station, to pay his superintendent a visit, as he was a great wretch. Many a young man had he drove to destruction. When I arrived at his place he was walking in front of his house. I rode up to him, and he bid me good evening. I dismounted and put a pistol to his head, saying, "If you move, I'll blow your head off!" All the men there was about the place was three. I ordered one of them to tie his hands behind him, and then to tie him to the verandah post. Then I went into the house and overhauled it. I found a single-barrel fowling piece and £4 in money. All the men seemed very pleased to serve him in the way I did. I now ordered one of the men to load my horse with things I wanted. I then untied him from the post, and ordered him to kneel down. "Oh, for God's sake, don't shoot me. I'll never get another man flogged if you forgive me this time." I forgave him, and I believe he behaved very kind to the men after that. I now mounted my horse and bid them good night, and left that part of the country.

I went to pay one of my friends a visit. When I came to his place I was treated with great kindness. I sent one of the females to a public house for some rum to regale ourselves. Someone that knew me saw me drinking there. This person went out and gave information, and I was taken when three parts drunk. They brought me to a public house sat Bungadore, where they confined me in the parlour with four men to guard me. Each man had a pistol. I rushed one of them, and took his pistol from him; the other three ran out of the door. I now had a run for it, but before I could reach the bush, I was surrounded with horsemen well-armed. I was brought back and secured in a curious manner. I had as many ropes and cords around me as a man could well carry, and so conveyed to gaol in a cart, tied up like a faggot.

In the course of two or three days I was taken before a magistrate, and committed for highway robbery. The magistrate who committed me was "Black Francis McCarty." He tried all he could to hang me by trying to make the witnesses swear to more than they knew. But I had the pleasure of taking satisfaction of him afterwards, as you shall hear in the course of your reading.

Prisoners' Barracks, Hyde Park. (1836)
Courtesy: Dixson Library, State Library of New South Wales, DL Pd 4; 9NaAKl2Y

Gidleigh, by Philip Gidley King (c.1840s)
Courtesy: National Library of Australia; PIC Drawer 2573 #R11133

2

More Bushranging

In the year 1841, on April 15, I was tried at Berrima for being in the bush under arms. I was found guilty, and transported for life to Norfolk Island, never to return. I remained in the gaol waiting to be conveyed down to Sydney. One morning the order came for me to go. I was placed in a cart and guarded by three mounted police and a constable. One night on the road I was placed in the lock-up at the Stone Quarry for the night. I put my wits to work to get out, and succeeded. I instantly made for the place where the mounted police slept. I took what arms I wanted, as they were all fast asleep. Next, I scaled the wall of the lock-up yard after a deal of trouble, for I was so heavily chained I could scarcely walk. Before I could get well into the bush, daylight made its appearance. I was surrounded by constables in all directions searching for me. I expected to be taken every minute. The thought came into my head to get up a tree. I picked out a good one, and scrambling up, there I remained all day. At night I came down, but dare not proceed any further, as the constables would be lying in wait all round me. I remained in this way for four days, up in the tree in the daytime, and down at night.

The fourth night I made to a house I could see some way off, to seek some refreshment and likewise something to cut my irons with. I knocked at the door, they opened it, and I went in. They all appeared to be very much frightened at my appearance. They were very poor people, and it grieved me to the heart to take anything from them. They gave me some refreshment, and I felt a different man altogether. I asked them for a knife and file to cut off my irons with. They gave them to me, and I bid them good night. I now walked into the bush, and cut my chains off that night. The next morning, I concealed myself under a bridge, waiting to stop the first man that came. In the course of an hour a gentleman came on horseback. I made my appearance in front of him with no hat and no shoes; all the clothes I had on was a shirt and a pair of trousers. I was something like a wild man, but I gave the old war cry, "Stand, or I'll blow your head off." I then ordered him off his horse, and to turn out his pockets. Then I mounted his horse, and marched him in the front of me a mile into the bush. I made him take off everything but his shirt. Then I put on his clothes and gave him my trousers; his own mother would hardly have known him. I told him I was going up the country, and bid him good day. After I had got out of sight, I turned my horse's head right round, and took down the country. I came on to the road and held gently along until I met two gentlemen going up the country. I stopped them, and took all their money and their watches. This job over I put spurs to my horse, and went lull gallop along, robbing everyone I met until I came to the Cow Pastures. Here I turned my horse adrift, as I did not consider I was safe on his back. He was dead beat. I then went to one of my friends to take a spell, and get some things I required.

The next place where I made my appearance was on the West End road, close to Paramatta. I stood by the road, and the first person I stuck up was a parson going to the West End church to preach. I did not rob him. I let him pass as he was a parson. I had an hour's conversation with him. He tried to get me to go to church with him, but that did not answer. A horse and chaise now made its appearance, and I bid the parson good day. When the horse and chaise came up to where I was standing, I ordered the driver to pull up or I would shoot him. I made him come down and empty his pockets. He was very loth to perform this part of the business but turned out about £27. I took also his coat and hat and let him go.

I did not fancy that part of the country, so I took the coach and went up towards Goulburn. Here I was in a part I knew well. I began again by sticking up Mr. H. I took all his money and his clothes, but I gave him mine in return. I then took him to a bridge and placed him underneath for about an hour. Three horsemen now made their appearance, all abreast and in earnest conversation. As they came near I jumped into the centre of the road with the word of command, made them get down and tie their horses to a tree. Then their pockets were turned out, and they stood back. I then advanced and took the money up. I then took Mr. J. M.'s horse and bid them good day.

One day as I came out on to the road, I saw some drays encamped. I tied my horse to a tree about 300 yards from the drays. I walked down to the drays. I knew one of the men. I asked him to make me a pot of tea. He told me I had better get off into the bush, as I was in danger there, five constables being with them looking for me only half an hour ago. I took his advice, and went back to my horse to wait while he brought me some tea and other refreshment, as he said he would. About five minutes after I had left the drays, I saw four mounted police come full gallop up to the drays. They did not stop there long, but came full speed towards me. My horse was unsaddled, with a tether rope round his neck, taking a feed of grass. I had no time for anything before they were upon me. I mounted a tree close to where my horse was tied, from which I had the pleasure of seeing them seeking for me for about an hour. They took my horse, but did not discover me. I got clean off, and they did not know how it was done.

I now thought the sooner I get a new horse the better; so, I made to Mr. Stukey's, to pay him a visit. I arrived at his place before he was up. When he made his appearance, I rather surprised him by telling him to stand. At this time there was no one up but himself. I went to the kitchen, and called the servant-man. He dressed himself, and came down stairs.
"Tie your master's hands behind him," I said. At this time all the young ladies came running down stairs in their nightgowns. "For God's sake, don't hurt my father," they cried. It seemed there was an ill-feeling between the servant-man and his master, as he had got him flogged a few days before. The servant-man now commenced pitching into his master, right and left; at which the young females appealed to me to prevent the servant from beating their father. I gave I the young ladies no answer to that, for I considered he was doing nothing but right.
The man now came to me and said, "Give me a pistol and I'll shoot him."
"No," I said, "I'll do no such thing."
I now over hauled the house. I found a double-barrelled gun. I then went into the kitchen and ordered the servant-woman to get breakfast ready. I then asked the master where the key of the store was. The servant-man took the key and unlocked the store. I went in, and found plenty of rum, wine, and brandy. I took a glass of the brandy, gave the servant-man one, and likewise the woman. I then asked the young ladies to take a glass of wine with me. This they did, and drank my health. After I had got such things as I required

out of the store, I took breakfast with Mr. and Mrs. Stukey. After breakfast I ordered Miss Stukey to go and bring me a suit of Mr. Stukey's best clothes. At this time the servant-man and also the servant-woman wanted to join me as companions. I gave my consent to the man, but not to the woman. He then put on a suit of his master's best clothes, while I went into the stable, saddled a horse, and put the plunder on his back. He was quite a young horse, and had not been rode many times. I mounted him, and off we went. The servant-woman came running after us and caught me by the hand. The horse took fright, and by chance flung me off and galloped away into the bush. I went back to Mr. Stukey's, and he begged and prayed of me not to let his servant-man go with me, as his time was almost done, and he promised me faithfully not to take him to court for his conduct that morning. I then advised the man to stay where he was, for mine was a very bad game to play. Having arranged my swag, I bid them good day, and was getting out of the paddock, when the female servant came running to me again, and catching hold of me said, "Where you go, I will go, so say no more." I tried to persuade her to go back, but she would not. So, I let her come with me, and a faithful companion she was whilst I remained in the bush.

I now thought I would pay my friend Mr. "Black Francis" McCarthy a visit. He was in the habit of going to Goulburn church every Sunday. I came to the road and waited. About 4 o'clock in the afternoon I saw him coming in his carriage. I was ready, and sprang out before them, and bid them pull up or be shot. I then ordered him down out of the carriage, and turn out his pockets, and be sharp about it, and not dare to speak one word to me, as he hadn't me in Goulburn Court-house now, and trying to make men swear away my life, and his life was now in my hands. It was my firm intention to tie him up to the wheel of his carriage, and make his driver flog him; but through his sister being with him he escaped this punishment. I next ordered him to take one of the horses out of the carriage and take off the harness, and I warned him that if he let the horse escape, I would consider he did it purposely, and blow his head off. When I had picked up the money and watch I got on the back of his carriage horse, and left him to his reflections. He was "black" enough when I met him, but I left him white enough; and from the top of a hill, I looked back and had the pleasure to see the coachman leading the one horse up the hill, and Mr. Black Francis pushing the carriage behind — a sight that gave me real satisfaction.

A view near Sydney, circa 1840s, by Viscountess Georgiana Lowe Sherbrooke. This is very alike the sort of views Westwood would have been familiar with in his bushranging days.
Courtesy: Mitchell Library, State Library of New South Wales; YzOgKBA9

View upon the Nepean River at the Cow Pastures, New South Wales, by Joseph Lycett (c.1825).
Courtesy: National Library of Australia; #U465 NK2707/18

3

Downfall

After this I again went up the country, and done several robberies on the other side of Goulburn, but the mounted police were soon in full chase of me, so I turned and went down until I got 100 miles, when I thought I would call and see Mr. Gray, who kept a large public house. I knew every room in this house, and where he kept his firearms.

One evening, just as it was getting dark, I tied my horse to a tree in the bush, and walked into the house. Mrs. Gray was behind the bar counter, and said, "Good evening, constable; have you heard any talk of Jacky Jacky, lately?"
"Yes, Mrs. Gray; I have heard of him up the country, and have been after him myself for the last month, but couldn't meet with him. A glass of rum if you please, Mrs. Gray; if Mr. Gray is in I want to see him."
"Go one of you," said Mrs. Gray, "and tell Mr. Gray a constable wants him."
When he came I wheeled round and gave the order "Bail up all; don't move hand or foot or I'll blow your brains out."

When I had bailed them all up, I went straight to Mr. Gray's bedroom and secured the arms, which made me master of the place. I also knew where the money was, and made Mrs. Gray pull out all the drawers in the chest. She pulled all out but one and it struck me she had her reasons for so doing, and I asked her why she didn't open that drawer.

"There's nothing in it, sir," she said; but I requested her to open it, and about £70 in silver and £20 in notes explained why the drawer was left last.

"Now, Mrs. Gray, take that drawer down to the bar', if you please, and empty what money there's in the till into it." This was done; and now I was master of all the cash as well as the arms in the house.

All the men I had bailed up stood in a passage a few yards in front of me. I now took up the drawer containing the money in my two hands, having first put the two guns I got in the bedroom under my arm; When I turned to go out of the front door, all the men rushed me, pinioned my arms behind my back. Then I saw what a mistake I had made in not making Mrs. Gray carry the drawer with the money outside; but it was too late. There were 12 or 14 men round me, as near as I can say, and although I had a tussle for it, I received a blow that knocked me down senseless, and when I came to myself, I found myself sectored in the taproom, with one end of a long chain round my neck, fastened with a padlock, and the other end made fast to a dray wheel laid in the middle of the room. There I remained all night like a monkey on a chain.

Next morning, I was placed in a cart with the chain made fast to the axletree, and in this conveyed to Berrima gaol. Shortly after I was removed, and conveyed to Sydney gaol in the year 1842. I was tried and convicted, and, with others, were transported for life to the penal settlement of Port Arthur, in Tasmania. Here I was associated with wretches of the foulest dye. It was their daily study to plunge one another into trouble.

I had not been long here when me and four others took the bush. After two days' wandering our leader brought us back to the spot we started from. In three days more, we were all captured, tried before the commandant, and received 100 lashes apiece for absconding. I was also put in irons, and my daily work was to carry a log of wood 1 cwt. up and down the settlement road. This continued about nine weeks, when one day the commandant released me, and sent me to gang with the other men.

Shortly afterwards I absconded again, to obtain what I had long been deprived of — liberty. Along with three other men I took the bush, with the intention of making a canoe. After being out several days with nothing to eat, we became quite weak. One morning I smelt a great smell, like the smell of meat roasting. We were more like hounds put on a scent, and seeking the hare. At last, we got to the sea, and there on the beach we saw a huge whale, dead, I should say, several days. It had been harpooned at sea, and washed in by the tide. It was this dead whale we had smelled. We were now supplied with meat in plenty, and subsisted on the flesh of it for several days while making our canoe. When it was almost finished the constables came on us and called on us to submit; but this was out of the question, and we ran for it, hoping they would fire on us and we should be shot, as death was preferable to life at Port Arthur at that time. After a short pursuit my companions were taken, but managed to give the constables the slip for some days longer; but I was taken, and the whole party were tried before Captain Booth, and each received 100 lashes, with heavy irons, and to be chained to a ringbolt while we were stone-breaking, and in a small room by night.

I remained in this way for nearly 12 months, when Captain Booth released me, and once more sent me to ordinary hard labour with the other men. About four months afterwards I took the bush once more, with two men who knew it well.

We got to the place agreed on, and where I could see the main land at about two miles distance. We must get across to it, and had no boat. I was a very bad swimmer. and two miles was a long pull for a new beginner. But my two companions did not hesitate, but pulled off their trousers and plunged into the water, with me after them, with my trousers thrown over my neck, for I was determined to get over to the mainland or be drowned in the attempt. After swimming about a mile, one of my companions — and very soon after the other — was seized, and drawn down by the sharks. I was left alone to the mercy of the waves, expecting the same fate every minute. At last, after a desperate struggle, I got to the land, but had lost my trousers and shirt, and scrambled ashore quite naked. In this state I found myself alone in a bush that I did not know, and greatly grieved at the death of my two companions. I made a bed in the long grass and picked up some shellfish that kept me alive for three days. On the fourth day the constables saw me, and I was brought back to Port Arthur once more, where I was punished with 90 days' solitary confinement and 12 months' "E.H.L.C." (extension with hard labour in chains).

After my 90 days' solitary was done things took a change. Captain Booth left Port Arthur, and Mr. Champ came Commandant, who treated me with great kindness; he took off my leg irons and removed me from the chain gang and soon placed me as servant to Mr. Laidley, the commissariat officer at Port Arthur, and a better master I never had. I was with him three months when I was promoted into the commandant's boat crew, and was going on well.

One day two gentlemen went out in their own boat to have a sail in the harbour, when they got capsized. The commandant's crew launched his boat and rescued them. In reward for this I and others were removed from Port Arthur to Hobart Town, and sent to Glenorchy probation station, which was a great advance. I was here six months when I felt a longing desire to see Sydney again, and me and Thos. Grilling and Wm. Allom agreed to take the bush. Allom was to be leader, as he said he knew the country. We got away, and after a whole day and night, the next morning our leader brought us back close to the station. I then took the lead, and the first place we stuck up was Mr. T. Y. Lowe's station to get arms. The next day was Sunday, and about dusk in the evening we stuck up Mr. White's, in Kangaroo Bottom, where we got a double and single barrel gun and two brace of pistols, by which we could now stand fight with the constables. We also took three suits of clothes and other things we wanted.

The very next morning a party of constables came across us, and shots were exchanged, one of which tore the pouch off a constable's belt, and it was a drawn battle. We now made for Brown's River, hoping to seize a small craft there, but were disappointed. We then headed up for New Norfolk, and four miles above it we stuck up a farm-house, beginning with the huts and ending with the house, from which we took a supply of things needful. Allom now turned right round, and would soon have got us among the constables, when I took the lead, and made for the Dromedary, where Martin Cash once took up his refuge.

From the top of this hill, we could see for miles round the country. Among the rocks we made up a fire, and with melted snow made tea and had our supper, for we were hungry, and tired, and cold.

Next day Allom again took the lead. But I soon saw that he did not know the country, and I had some sharp words with him for deceiving us before we bolted by bragging of his acquaintance with it. We were very uncomfortable, a sign that misfortune was near. I took the lead through a thick scrub, but soon after I missed Gilling, for whom I had a sincere regard, and I called a halt for him to come up. After waiting a long time, I set to look for him, and cooeyed as loud as I dare; but I never saw him again. He sent me word afterwards, when he was lying under sentence in Launceston gaol, that he lost us by accident in taking a wrong turn, and was afraid to cooey.

Towards evening I and Allom made for the township or Green Ponds, and, after pitching on a place to camp in, Allom set out for the village to get some things we wanted. After waiting for him five or six hours I began to think he had fallen in with the constables, for he never came back. He was a resolute man, and had many good qualities; but he deceived me in saying he knew the bush of Tasmania. He told me afterwards, when I met him a prisoner in Norfolk Island, that he left me because he was afraid I would shoot him; but such a thing never entered my mind, and I always had a fear of shedding blood, though I often spoke rough to people I stuck up. When I found that Allom did not return, I was quite cast down. I was left to myself; ignorant of the country, hungry and tired, constables on the alert at all the townships, my comrades lost, and no hope of getting to the coast and escape.

I spent a very miserable night after Allom's departure, and next day pushed on by myself to the Lovely Banks, where I was seen and challenged by a constable, who called on me to surrender. This roused me, and, levelling my gun at him, I ordered him to throw down his piece or I'd blow his head off. To my great astonishment he threw it down, at the first word. I bid him stand back, and then I took up his gun and fired it off, and rifled him of his ammunition. I was going to break his gun, but he begged hard of me to give it back to him, and did so and let him go. Yet this cowardly fellow afterwards swore in court that I fired five shots at him when I never fired at him at all.

I got some food at a house, and the second day after my encounter with the constable I reached Oatlands, but I was now too dejected to go any further. My lightness of heart, that never failed me before, now deserted me. At sundown I turned off the road some way and lighted a fire to have some refreshment, and then lay down to sleep very unhappy, and indifferent whether I ever woke again.

Next morning a stockman passing early through the bush saw me, and gave information to the constables at Oatlands police station, and I was soon surrounded by four of them well armed, captured, and sent down handcuffed to Hobart Town, where I was tried at the next assizes, and for the third time sentenced to transportation for life, and now with 10 years' detention at Norfolk Island.

Port Arthur penal settlement with the commissariat store prominent at the water's edge. (c.1871)
Courtesy: Libraries Tasmania; LPIC102/1/67

"Green Pons (Ile Van Diemen)" [Green Ponds (Van Diemen's Land)] by L. Lebreton and P. Blanchard (c.1841).
Courtesy: National Library of Australia; #S11301

A Postscript by "Peutetre"

The foregoing was, in fact, written by Westwood, on my suggestion. To a sanguine and nervous temperament like his, a Norfolk Island cell was as irksome as stable and halter to a zebra of the Zulu deserts. He could read pretty well; but he soon wearied of it, and sought relief for his restlessness in an attempt to break out of "prison thrall." But the strong stone walls and solid flooring of freestone blocks of the new octagon gaol might defy the industry of Trenck himself.

There was, however, a vulnerable point. The ceiling of the cells was only wooden planks, two inches thick, and 13ft. from the ground. Westwood resolved that the ceiling should be cut through, though the gaol authorities supplied neither step ladder or saw. A step ladder was dispensed with by his standing on the shoulders of a fellow prisoner confined in the same cell; a saw was smuggled into his hands by a confederate employed about the gaol. This "saw" was an instrument once well renown at Tasmanian penal stations and at Norfolk Island. It was of steel, about three or four inches long, easily carried and concealed. With one of these, and elevated on his cell mate's neck, he cut away cautiously and painfully for a fortnight at the wooden ceiling.

The gaol was only one story high. If a hole were made in the ceiling the shingles of the roof could be removed by the hand, and egress secured. But to get clear off, he must creep along the roof to the boundary wall at the risk of being shot by the military sentry within the gaol; and if he jumped down he was almost sure to drop into the grasp of the patrol constable outside; and if he could evade these difficulties and get into the lemon groves, their densest thicket and deepest gully could afford him a hiding-place and freedom only for a day. Yet, for this one day's exemption from convict "chains and slavery," he would gladly saw his anxious road through the ceilings of all the cells in the gaol.

A prisoner in a next cell overheard the sawing, and hinted to the gaoler that there was "something up" in Westwood's cell. The result was that turnkeys came and surprised him when he had well nigh completed his opening in the ceiling, removed him to another, and placed him in heavier fetters.

For some days he was in great perturbation at being detected, and to turn his thoughts into a calmer channel, I recommended him to ask for paper and write his life. The idea seemed to please him. I knew it would be slow and tedious employment for him. But he got the paper, commenced writing, and there was no more trouble with him. The end of his story is told in my introductory remarks.

P.

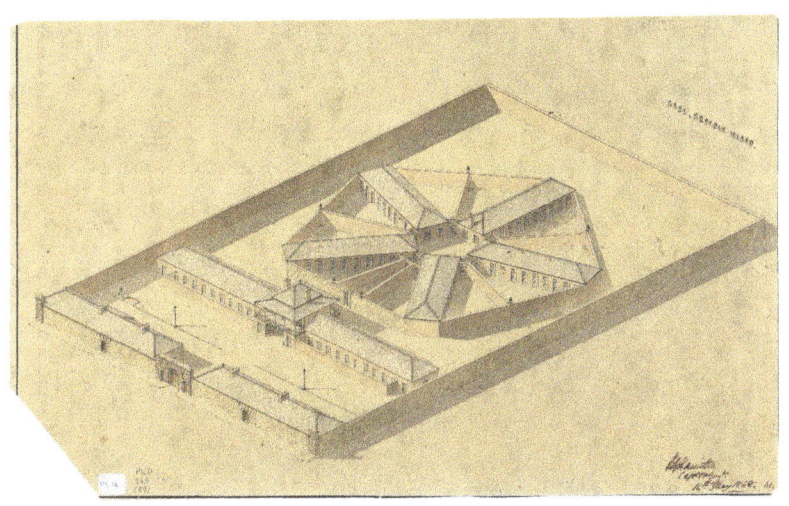

Norfolk Island - Gaols (c.1837)
*Courtesy: Libraries Tasmania, Public Works Department
(TA24); PWD266/1/1891*

Alexander Maconochie, the former /commandant of Norfolk Island whose beneficial innovations were discarded by his incumbent Major Joseph Childs in favour of a more punitive approach.
Courtesy: Libraries Tasmania, PH30/1/2026

The Cooking Pot Riot

It is impossible to convey the story of William Westwood without going into some detail regarding the so-called "Cooking Pot Riot" that resulted in his execution. Not only is the event remarkable in the life of Westwood for its brutality, it is perhaps more notable for its incongruity with his prior behaviour.

The following is a contemporary news report that related the events of the riot to people on the Australian mainland. At the time it was printed, the trials of the rioters were still yet to be concluded. It was republished in numerous publications without alteration, and so it is here reproduced in full with the appropriate typographical errors amended.

(From a Correspondent of the Sydney Morning Herald)

We have been recently favoured with important intelligence from this island, and as it is but rarely any of the doings of that unhappy spot reach the public ear or eye, we are glad to have it in our power to communicate an account of the late proceedings upon which our readers may fully rely. A more melancholy one can scarcely be imagined, and if to what we now publish we were to add other enormities with which we have been made acquainted, we can scarcely doubt but that the whole community would indignantly protest against a station which, it may be feared will sooner or later call down the vengeance of God, as of old, upon the nation which can tolerate such a festering mass of wickedness. The late Commandant it was universally confessed, was unfitted in every possible way for the duties most unaccountably entrusted to him.

The following may be relied upon as a correct outline of the late transactions; and of the incentives which terminated in so frightful and so fatal a tragedy.

From a state of really quiet obedience; the island, from the time of the prisoners (who are not. slow to appreciate character) began to perceive the weakness of the Superintendent, fell into a gradually increasing state of insubordination. Some of the prisoners cringed, others plotted, and others bullied him. Temporary expedients were resorted to, in order to keep them quiet, but all discipline was relaxed, and when the difficulty of managing them became daily greater and the various officers remonstrated, their complaints were either treated with rudeness, or altogether evaded. To make matters worse, an increasing number of ruffians began to be landed from Van Diemens Land, who soon rendered the English prisoners as mischievous as themselves. What a state of things! An absolute ruler! yet thoroughly incapable; at war with every officer on the island, bearded by the convicts, and at length in open day knocked down by one of them. It would occupy too much time to tell of the progressive steps by which the total insubordination of the convicts, and the disorganisation of all system were brought about.

Mutinous disturbances began towards the close of last year. The ration of the prisoners has always been notoriously bad at Norfolk Island — throughout the year they have salt beef and maize meal only, so that but for the indulgence (always allowed them) of growing a few sweet potatoes in plots of ground marked out for their use and cultivated by themselves on Saturday afternoons, their fare would have been positively destructive of life, as indeed it frequently proved to the freshly arrived prisoners, before they could grow potatoes for themselves. On the 1st of January, a public order was posted to the effect, that all their garden plots were henceforth to be taken away from them. It is difficult for any person unacquainted with the island to conceive the commotion this occasioned. The prisoners refused to work unless some equivalent were given for the potatoes, and after some hesitation, which only rendered matters worse, a hall pint of pease was promised each man daily. At the end of three or four days the pease were said to be all issued, and there was another row. The Superintendent then promised to have 8 oz. of 12 percent, flour served out in lieu of the pease, To add to this unhappy state of affairs, a resident Police Magistrate had been appointed from Van Diemen's Land, who very soon rendered himself an object of vengeance. The flogging became perfectly furious, from 500 to nearly 2000 lashes were inflicted of a morning, until the ground about the triangles was literally soaked with human blood.

Matters daily grew worse, the wretched men by this sort of alternate rage and peevish vacillation gradually grew more and more exasperated and insubordinate. About the commencement of June the store of flour was reported by the Commissariat officer to be nearly exhausted, and as a matter of course the 8 oz. of flour were discontinued. The men became more clamorous than ever By an order published in May 1845, and forming part of the Van Diemen's Land Regulations for Norfolk Island, it had been announced that the gardens being no longer allowed, 2 lbs, of sweet potatoes should form a part of the daily ration to each prisoner. It will scarcely be credited that Major Childs caused this order to be posted at every station on the island; yet knowing at the time he did so, that it was impossible to furnish the men with a single ounce daily potatoes! During fourteen months this order had been hanging up before the men's eyes! They read it, and again and again demanded their allowance of vegetables, they promised, but withheld from them: and when at length they became furious and riotously clamorous, they were told that it had been determined by a board that 2 oz. of salt pork was equivalent to 8 oz of flour! (the ration issued instead of peas); and that this, would be accordingly issued to them instead of the 2 lbs of sweet potatoes, to which, under the regulations, they were entitled.

It is utterly impossible to conceive the state of mind in which the men are described to have been at this time; such trifling had really goaded them to the point of madness; they were ready for any desperate deed, and the deed alas! was too soon effected. Ever since the time of Major Anderson, the prisoners had been allowed for each mess a tin pot to cook the potatoes. &c., in. It was suggested by the stipendary magistrate that it would form a powerful effect on the minds of the men — a new stage our penal science, in short powerfully reformatory in every way, if these abominable kettles, (in which more mischief was supposed to be brewed than ever Macbeth's Witches ever dreamt of) were taken away, and therefore simultaneously with an order, announcing that at length the long expected 2 lbs. of potatoes would be issued; it was added that on the evening previous to the 1st July, all their kettles would be seized.

This order was acted upon in a manner which showed the men that the hand of authority trembled in the execution of its duty. When all the prisoners were shut up in their wards, except the few who attended school, the police went into the lumber yard, and look away the obnoxious kettles, and every thing belonging to the prisoners they could find. At this time "Jackey Jackey" (William Westwood, of some notoriety in this colony) was sitting in school, about seven o'clock, when a hand-cart came rattling into the barrack-yard, and a crash of tin vessels was heard. Jackey Jackey was busy in the intricacies of a sum at this moment, he suddenly paused — lifted up his hand with the pencil in it, held it elevated for a few seconds, as it listening and hesitating — then dashed down the pencil — pushed the slate off the table with a violent movement — and deliberately folding his arms, as if he had finally made up his mind, remained buried in thought the rest of the evening. Every man followed his example, and sat whispering until the school broke up.

The following morning the men were all mustered for prayers — a practice but recently introduced — (nothing can be more disgraceful than the former negligence in this respect) and during the service a murmuring sort of sound was heard passing from bench to bench. It has since been surmised that this was a signal for the indiscriminate slaughter of the officers present; but nothing was at that time attempted. After prayers they all went into the lumber yard and found the tins gone. A short pause ensued, and then they all marched back again, five or six deep, to the Barrack yard in perfect silence — broke into the store, took out every vessel in it, and returned in the same manner to the lumber yard. As they approached, Jackey Jackey addressed his followers in a speech. "Now, my men," said he, "I've made up my mind to bear this oppression no longer; but, remember, I'm going to the gallows, if any man therefore funks; let him stand out of the way! Come on." A loud cheer followed from his desperate followers. A policeman named Morris was in the archway, Jackey Jackey, with an immense bludgeon, others with sticks, one man with a reaping hook, and another with a pitchfork, rushed upon the unhappy man, and knocked him down, he struggled, and got into the room behind him. Jackey Jackey followed him, and beat his head to pieces. The men, furious by the taste of blood, then proceeded to the cookhouse, where Stephen Smith, the police runner, was. The same murderous villain rushed on him also; then poor Smith, who was formerly much liked by the prisoners, cried out most piteously, "for God's sake don't hurt me, Jackey ! remember my poor wife and children !" "D— n your wife and children" was the horrible reply, accompanied by a blow which beat in poor Smith's eye, and the side of his face. His shrieks for help, were terrific; but in a second or two his cries were over for ever. From the cookhouse they proceeded to the Police house at the Baarack-gate [sic] At the corner of the road, Price, overseer of work, and a man named Ingram, were standing, Jackey Jackey made a furious rush at Price, and aimed a deadly blow at him, but Price stooped, and the blow fell upon Ingram, nearly killing him. The mob came rushing on with such violence, that Westwood was pushed forward, and Price escaped, he knows not how, and ran for the soldiers.

The great object of the mob at this time seems to have been to seize the stipendiary magistrate, Mr. Barrow, who usually sat at six o'clock every morning to try cases.

Most providentially he was this morning on a board of survey, and so escaped. The beach guard seeing the mob approaching, advanced, and forming near the gaol, drove the rioters back. They then ran towards Government House, and on their way Westwood stopped at the lime-kiln, and entered the hut there with an axe; which he had by this time obtained. Two policemen, Dillon and Saxton, were in bed. The former was actually asleep when the cowardly villain drove in his skull by a blow of the axe, and Saxton only opened his eyes to see his death-blow fall from the hand of the same monster; the wounds were most appalling ones — the walls of the room were scattered with brains and blood.

Westwood, after this atrocity, coolly lighted his pipe, and, after a few puffs, shouted out, "Now for the Christ killer," and a cry was immediately raised, "To Barrow's, to Barrow's." Happily the alarm given by Price had roused the military, who were now under arms, and at this critical juncture, the soldiers were seen running down the Water-road: the rioters instantly retreated to the lumber yard — Westwood loudly denouncing their cowardice. The place was surrounded, and after much difficulty and delay, the ringleaders were seized, and about sixty left to be tried by a special Court of Criminal Sessions.

So rests for the present this fearful tragedy, unparalleled in heartless atrocity. How much, of its guilt may be justly traced to the hands and heads to which the supreme authority was entrusted, it is hard to say; but never was a greater blunder committed, or one which has been followed by more disastrous consequences, than the appointment of the late Superintendent to a post requiring so much intelligence and firmness, tempered indeed by an enlightened humanity. We ardently hope that discipline may be restored end sounder principles be acted upon. Without extenuating in the most remote degree the enormities of which the diabolical perpetrators of these atrocities have been guilty, we must still commiserate the fate of better men whose feelings hare been insulted, who have been bullied and trifled with, harrassed [sic] and cheated by men who may boast of their savings, but who will not soon shake off the odium of their doings. We trust again, we say, that order may be established in this, after all, most horrible plague spot; but it is to be feared, that like the tiger which has once drunk blood, it will be long before these wretched men, cooped up so unnaturally, and lacerated in mind and body, will forget the power for mischief they have discerned by these acts they really possess.

"Cooking pot riot, Kingston, Norfolk Island, 1 July, 1846" by unknown artist.
Courtesy: Launceston Local Studies Collection, Tasmanian Archive and Heritage Office; SD_ILS:110913

The Letters

In the last days of Westwood's life, he made sure to record his final thoughts in letters dictated from the condemned cell at Norfolk Island. What follows are transcripts of those letters, including a verbatim portion that Westwood wrote personally in a letter to his family. These letters were published by the press of the time.

In a commentary on Westwood's letter to his parents from the *Britannia and Trades' Advocate* of 29 April 1847, the remarkable nature of these letters was described:

In a former number we gave the copy of a letter written by William Westwood, better known as Jackey Jackey, and at the time of its appearance an attempt was made to shew that he had died breathing a spirit of bitterness very unsuited to any man at the last hour of his existence. What the motives for doing Westwood such an injustice, it is not our present purpose to inquire; certain however it is, that such was not the fact, as the following copy of another letter will show. "Justice to free and bond" is our maxim in such matters, and we see no reason why the last dying thoughts of the malefactor should not be as fairly represented as those of him whose life has not been forfeited to the offended laws of his country.

Westwood, although an illiterate person, was a man of strong natural abilities; those enabled him to dictate every word of the following address, to a fellow prisoner, who wrote them down for him, as his (Westwood's) thoughts flowed; but the signature, and what may be considered the postscript, were written by himself.

4

A Farewell to Family

Norfolk Island, South Pacific Ocean, 12th October, 1846.

My dear Father and Mother, — Heaven knows I have neglected you, to whom I owe so many kindnesses, and have in my youth acted contrary to your wishes, and parental instructions; thus it follows, that it is now my lot to address you whom I love dearly, under such distressing and to you as well as myself, such painful circumstances. You have, I am sure, had many unhuppy moments respecting me; but I now must endeavour to prepare you for a shock, which I am afraid will be almost more than you can or will be able to endure. But, my dear parents, brothers, and sisters, mourn not for me, I who long before you can possibly receive his will have been ushered into the awful presence of his Maker, and will have appeared before that great Tribunal of Justice, where all must render an account for their actions, where all hearts are open, and where all secrets are known: — therefore I say, my dear relations, mourn not for me, but let my unfortunate lot be a lesson to the living, let the younger branches of our family, and the offspring of them, learn to honour their fathers, and mothers in their youth; for neglecting those precepts, these holy and heavenly laws, has brought me to the situation I now am placed in; but it is, it must be the work of that great God who made heaven and earth, and all that therein is, and who knows all things; for it is now, and only now, that I see my error; it is now only I can see and know the multitude of God's mercies towards me, it is now I am brought to a right sense of my duty towards Him, and it is now I can repeat, as applicable to my own case, these beautiful words of the Psalmist—

The wonders he for me has wrought shall fill my mouth with songs of praise and others to his worship brought, To hopes of like deliverance raise. *40th Psalm, 3rd verse.*

No sooner I my wound disclosed; The guilt that tortur'd me within, But thy forgiveness interposed, And mercy's healing balm poured in. *32nd Psalm, 5th verse.*

I can now, my dear and beloved parents, withhold the truth of my fate no longer from you; for an outbreak took place at this ill-fated settlement on the 1st day of July last, when some lives were lost, for which I have been tried and condemned to die, — which sentence will be carried into effect before the setting of tomorrow's sun. Bear this with humble fortitude, for I at first made up my mind not to write at all, but then I thought you might perchance see the account in the public press, and I know it would be a great satisfaction to you, even under such trying and truly heart-rending circumstances, to hear, and that from myself, that I died as a Christian, embracing the same faith as I was taught when a child, putting my whole trust and confidence in Christ Jesus, who shed his blood in ignominy for me and all repenting sinners; through his blood alone

I can and must be saved: he heard the prayers of the dying thief upon the cross, and through his faith forgave his sins even at the eleventh hour. During this time or trial and affliction, I have been attended by the Rev. Thomas Rogers, of the Church of England, to which gentleman I owe everything; his attention to me has been unceasing; night and day has he laboured to bring me to a right sense of my duty towards an offended Maker. May that God whom he has taught me to fear and love, reward him ten thousand fold!

Dearly beloved parents, give my kind love and affection to my dear brothers and sisters; tell them, I trust and earnestly hope my disgraceful and unfortunate untimely end will be an everlasting barrier against their ever doing evil; tell them, with you to bear up against this unhappy occurrence, and endeavour to spend their lives in such a way as will ensure a peaceful death.

I again entreat you all not to mourn for me, for through Christ Jesus, and a hearty and sincere repentence; I hope to meet you all in the realms of everlasting bliss. May God bless you; may He be with you, may He guide your steps; direct your hearts, and in the end may he receive your never-dying souls into his mansion of everlasting happiness and peace, is the earnest and sincere prayers of your unfortunate and dying son.

William Westwood.

Dear pearants, I send you a piece of my hear in remberance of me, your son, Wm. Westwood. Good Bye, and God Bless you all.

5

The Last Letter

H. M. Gaol, Norfolk Island,
Condemned Cells, 1846, Oct. 3

REVEREND SIR, — As in duty bound to you for the kindness you have shewn to me, and the interest I have always seen you take in those that have ever been under your spiritual care, whatever may be their fate, I have been induced to write to you, hoping this may find you in good health, and in the enjoyment of all God's choicest blessings. I have to inform you that long before this letter reaches your hands, the hand that wrote this will be cold in death. I do not grieve that the hour is fast approaching that is to end my earthly career. I welcome death as a friend; — the world, or what I have seen of it, has no allurements in it for me. 'Tis not for me to boast; but yet, Sir, allow a dying man to speak a few words to one who has always shewn a sympathy for the wretched outcasts of society, and ever, with a Christian charity, strove to recall the wretched wanderer to a sense of his lost condition. I started in life with a good feeling for my fellow-man. Before I well knew the responsibility of my station in my life, I had forfeited my birthright. I became a slave, and was sent far from my dear native country, my parents, my brothers, and sisters — torn from all that was dear to me, and that for a trifling offence. Since then I have been treated more like a beast than a man, until nature could bear no more. I was, like many others, driven to despair by the opresive and tyrannical conduct of those whose duty it was to prevent us from being treated in this way. Yet these men are courted by society ; and the British Government deceived by the interested representations of those men, continue to carry on a system that has and still continues to ruin the prospects of the souls and bodies of thousands of British subjects. I have not the ability to represent what I feel on the subject, yet I know from my own feelings that it will never carry out the wishes of the British people! The spirit of the British law is reformation. Now, years of sad experience should have told them, that instead of reforming the wretched man, under the present system, led by example on the one hand, and driven by despair and tyranny on the other, goes on from bad to worse; till at length he is ruined body and soul.

Experience, dear-bought experience has taught me this. In all my career, I never was cruel – I always felt keenly for the miseries of my fellow creatures, and was ever ready to do all in my power to assist them to the utmost, yet my name will be handed down to posperity [sic] branded with the most opprobrious epithet that man can bestow. But 'tis little matter now. I have thus given vent to my feelings, knowing that you will bear with me, and I know that you have and will exert yourself for the welfare of wretched men. It is on this account that I have strove, though in but a feeble manner, to express my feelings. The crime for which I am to suffer is murder. Revd. Sir, you will shudder at my cruelty, but I only took life — those that I deprived of life, tho' they did not in a moment send a man to his last account, inflicted on many a lingering death – for years they have tortured men's minds as well as their bodies, and after years of mortal and bodily torture sent them to a premature grave. This is what I call refined cruelty, and it is carried on, and I blush to own it, by Englishmen, and under the enlightened British Government. Will it be believed hereafter, that this was allowed to be carried on in the nineteenth century?

I will now proceed to inform you what has happened to me since I left Port Arthur. I was sent to Glenorchy probation station. I was then determined if possible to regain my freedom, and visit my dear native country, and see my parents and friends again. I took the bush, with two men; one of them said that he knew the bush well, but he deceived me and himself too. Our intention was to take a craft from Brown's River ; we were disappointed — there was no craft there. We then turned to go to Launceston, thinking to get one there, and to cross to the Sydney main. But after leaving New Norfolk, I lost one of my mates, and the same night the other left me at the Green Ponds. I was soon after taken and sent to Hobart Town. I was tried, and sent to Norfolk Island, and this place is now worse than I can describe. Every species of petty tyranny that long experience has taught some of these tyrants, is put in force by the authorities. The men are half-starved, hard-worked, and cruelly flogged.

These things brought on the affair of the first of July, of which you have no doubt heard. I would send you the whole account, but that I know you will have it from better hands than mine. I am sorry that this will give you great pain, as there are several of the men that have been under your charge at Port Arthur concerned in this affair. Sir, on the 21st of September, 1846, Mr. Brown arrived in the Island with a commission to form a Court, and try the men.

On the 23rd of September he opened the Court, fourteen men were then arraigned for the murder of John Morris, that was formerly gate keeper at Port Arthur. This trial occupied the Court nine days. The jury retired, and returned a verdict, and found twelve out of fourteen guilty of murder. On the 5th of October the sentence of death was then passed on us, and to be carried into effect on the 13th of October, 1846. Sir, the strong ties of earth will soon be wrenched, and the burning fever of this life will soon be quenched, and my grave will be a haven — a resting place for me, William Westwood. Sir, out of the bitter cup of misery, I have drank from my sixteenth year — ten long years, — and the sweetest draught is that which takes away the misery of living death; it is the friend that deceives no man ; all will then be quiet — no tyrant will then disturb my repose, I hope, William Westwood.

Sir, I now bid the world adieu, and all it contains,
WM. WESTWOOD, his writing.

6

The Dying Declaration of William Westwood, alias "Jackey Jackey."

"I, William Westwood, wish to die in the Communion of Christ's Holy Church, seeking mercy of God through Jesus Christ our Lord and Saviour. — Amen.

"I wish to say, as a dying man, that I believe four men now going to suffer are innocent of the crime laid to their charge, viz :— Lawrence Kavenagh, Henry Whiting, William Pickthorne, and William Scrimshaw. I declare that I never spoke to Kavenagh on the morning or the riots; and these other three men had no part in the killing of John Morris as far as I know of. I have never spoke a disrespectful word of any man since my confinement. I die in charity with all men, and now I ask your prayers for my soul!

William Westwood, Aged 26 years."

The Fate of William Westwood (as reported)

The following two reports come from The Courier (Hobart) and portray the news of the rioters on Norfolk Island as it was conveyed by ship from the island at the time. They are presented here to show William Westwood's fate following the riot as those contemporary to him would have learned it. It contextualises all of which you have read in this book prior to this in very straightforward terms.

***

Wednesday 28 October 1846, page 3

NORFOLK ISLAND.

THE *Lady Franklin* arrived yesterday morning, bringing intelligence of considerable interest. She had as passengers, the following officers, who have been suspended by Mr. Price, the Civil Commandant:— Mr. Gilbert Robertson, Superintendent of the Agricultural Department; Mr. Fraser, one of the Assistant-Superintendents; and

Overseers Kelly, Lawler, and Smithers. We have not learnt the several causes of suspension.

The criminal sessions had not closed when the Franklin sailed. The general rumour, we need hardly say, is incorrect, of the officers of the Court having returned. As principals in the riots, and the murders of Smith, Morris, and others, fourteen prisoners were tried. Of these twelve were found guilty and two acquitted. Of the twelve found guilty, and sentenced to die, were William Westwood, (the well known bushranger in New South Wales, and in this colony by the name of "Jackey Jackey,") and Lawrence Kavenagh, the associate of Cash and Jones in this colony.

The twelve men found guilty of the riots and murders were executed on the morning of Tuesday, October 13. Six of them expiated their offences on the scaffold at eight in the morning, and the other six at ten o'clock on the same day.

The scene has been described to us, by eye-witnesses, as one of most awful solemnity. All the men died penitent.

***

Saturday 31 October 1846, page 2

NORFOLK ISLAND.

In the last *Courier* we gave a brief notice of the execution, at Norfolk Island, of twelve men who (with two others acquitted) had been tried and found guilty of the murder of John Morris, a constable, at the period of the riots. Several other murders were committed, in which the prisoners were implicated, but a conviction having followed with regard to the murder of Morris, the other informations were not proceeded with.

The twelve unhappy men were executed on the morning of the 13th October. Three of them had been brought up in the Protestant faith, and were attended on the scaffold by the Rev. Mr. Rogers, one of the Episcopalian chaplains of the island. The other nine men, being of the Roman Catholic faith, were attended in their last moments by the Rev. Messrs. Murray and Bond. The three Protestants were, William Westwood, *alias* Jackey Jackey, Henry Whiting, and William Pickthorne. It forms a remarkable feature in these trials, that Jackey Jackey, in his last moments, made the following declaration to the clergyman by whom he was attended :— "I wish to say, as a dying man, that I believe four men now going to suffer, are innocent of the crime laid, to their charge, viz. — Lawrence Kavenagh, Henry Whiting, William Pickthorne, and William Scrimshaw, and declare that I never spoke to Kavenagh on the morning of the riots; and these other three men had no part in the killing of John Morris, as far as I know of." Two of the men mentioned by Jackey Jackey made solemn declarations of their innocence. Jackey Jackey was 26 years of age, Henry Whiting 22, and William Pickthorne 27. Whiting and five others were formerly of the crime class, Point Puer, Port Arthur. Jackey Jackey left with the clergyman who attended him a long written history of his career, of which we have seen a copy. He did not deny his guilt of the crime for which he was about to suffer. We have only space for the concluding portion of this document, which is evidently much worse written than the preceding part; it bears evidence of the culprit having laboured, at the time, under strong emotion. We give the extract verbatim. It was written in the condemned cell.

" Sir the strong tyes of earth will soon be wrentched and the burning fever of this life will soon be quentched and my grave will be a heavens — a resten place for me Wm. Westwood. Sir out of the Bitter cup of misery — I have drank from my sixteenth year 10 long years, and the sweetest draught is that which takes away the misery of living death — it is the friend that deceives no man — all will then be quiet no tyrant will disturb my repose I hope — Wm. Westwood."

" Sir I know bid the world adiue and all it contains."

"Wm. Westwood his wrighting."

On the morning of the day when the *Franklin* sailed another man was executed for a murder at the Lime Kilns, but we believe this crime did not arise out of the general riots and other murders.

It is said that Martin Cash, the former associate of Lawrence Kavenagh, is a very well-conducted man, and has gained general esteem.

Six other men had been sentenced to die. The Court was sitting when the *Franklin* sailed.

Murderer's Mound, Norfolk Island: William Westwood's final resting place.
Courtesy: Libraries Tasmania, PH8/1/33

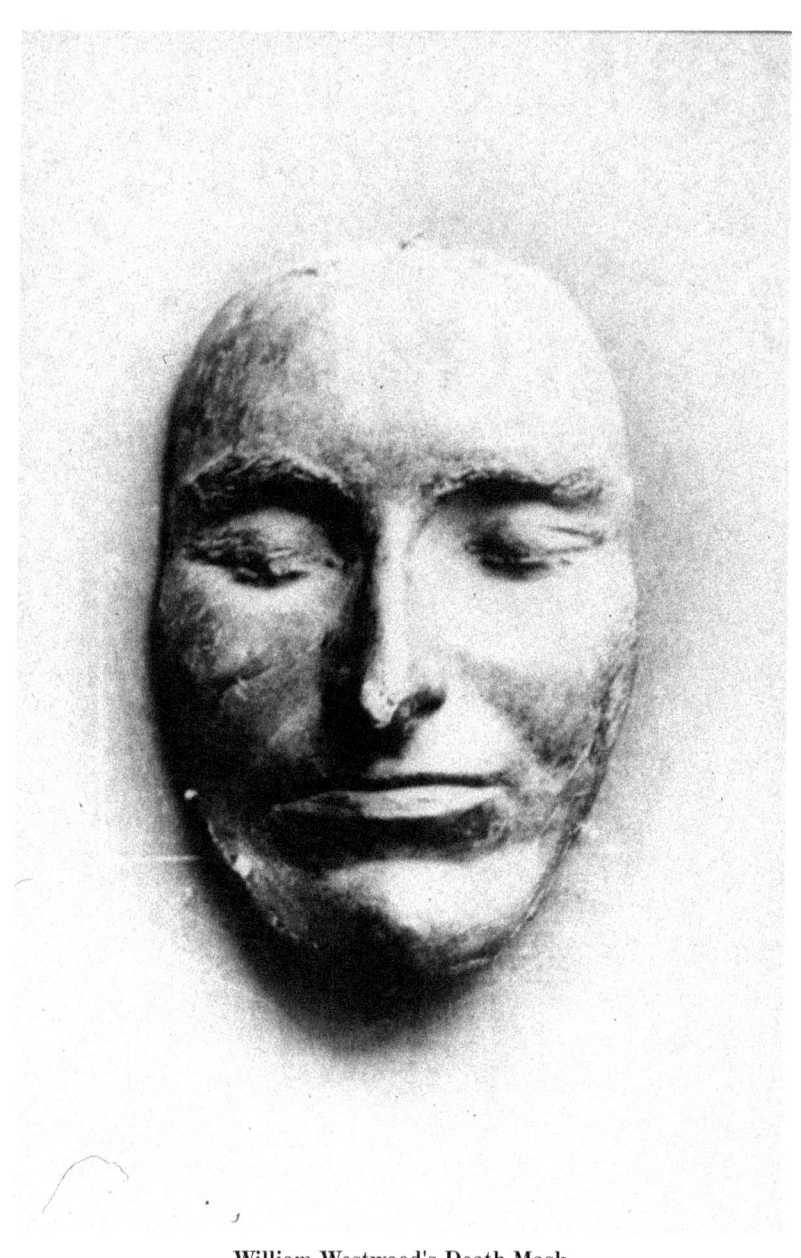

William Westwood's Death Mask
*Courtesy: Mitchell Library, State Library of New South Wales,
2 - 52019; 1l4PZVz1*

The Author

William Westwood was only sixteen when he was transported as a convict in 1837 for stealing a coat. After landing in New South Wales he was assigned to work at Gidleigh Station under a cruel overseer and master, who would have him flogged at any opportunity. In response to this he became a bushranger, engaging in various acts of highway robbery, during which time he gained his nickname, "Jackey Jackey". Westwood had a knack for evading his pursuers and escaping from his captors, which led to him being imprisoned in the harshest prisons in Australia, including Port Arthur and Norfolk Island.

In 1846, aged twenty-six, he was hanged for murder after killing four men during a riot on Norfolk Island. Prior to his death he wrote a short autobiography and a series of letters that have been reproduced in this book.

The Editor

Aidan Phelan is the writer and historian for *A Guide to Australian Bushranging*, an online resource that has been bringing Australia's outlaw heritage to a worldwide audience since 2017. In 2020 he published his first novel, *Glenrowan*, which depicts the final months of the Kelly Gang's outlawry through to Ned Kelly's execution, based on his historical research. In 2022 he released two non-fiction books, *Aaron Sherritt: Persona non Grata*, and *Bushranging Tales: Volume One*.

Aidan has a Bachelor of Arts and a Diploma of Education, but also studied writing and editing at what is now known as Melbourne Polytechnic. He was born and raised in the suburbs of Melbourne and developed a fascination with the story of Ned Kelly on his first visit to Glenrowan as a child. He has also worked as an illustrator and regularly provides illustrations for *An Outlaw's Journal* by Georgina Stones. He is also developing *Glenrowan* as a miniseries for television and streaming with Matthew Holmes (writer and director of *The Legend of Ben Hall*).